Itch Like Crazy

VOLUME 51

SUN TRACKS

AN AMERICAN INDIAN LITERARY SERIES

Itch Like Crazy

WENDY ROSE

THE UNIVERSITY OF ARIZONA PRESS

TUCSON

The University of Arizona Press
© 2002 Wendy Rose
First Printing
All rights reserved

♽ This book is printed on acid-free, archival-quality paper.
Manufactured in the United States of America

Library of Congress Cataloging-in-Publication Data
Rose, Wendy.
Itch like crazy / Wendy Rose.
p. cm. — (Sun tracks ; v. 51)
ISBN 0-8165-2177-8 (acid-free paper)
1. Family—Poetry. 2. Racially mixed people—Poetry.
3. Indians of North America—Poetry. I. Title. II. Series.
PS501 .S85 vol. 51
[PS3568.O7644]
810.8 s—dc21
[811/.
2002006441

British Library Cataloguing-in-Publication Data
A catalogue record for this book is available from the British Library.

Publication of this book is made possible in part by the proceeds
of a permanent endowment created with the assistance of a
Challenge Grant from the National Endowment for the Humanities,
a federal agency.

For the Grandmothers I still seek;
for the daughter who almost lived.
And for Tiny, Sayan, Miguel, and Leiminda,
without whose kindness
these poems would never have been written.
Finally,
for the young bald eagle who blessed Arthur and me
by allowing us to witness his first flight
behind our house.

Contents

PART 2: THIS HEART

PART 3: LISTEN HERE FOR THE VOICES

Itch Like Crazy

PART ONE

These Bones

Imagine it like this.

In the middle of the sea, there is a place
of ghosts and transformation.
When the people who lived to the east of magic
began to itch and hurt
feeling fear
and, icicles running
the length of their faces, they shed
freezing tears
and were drawn to the place of transformation
with the frenzy of moths
drawn to fire.
They believed in their own powerlessness so deeply,
lived in the ruins their leaders had made,
dipped their newborn babes in polluted and dangerous water
because it was thought they were born already in sin.
Seeking redemption
in the water they had polluted,
they let the northern fog and the ocean take them
and only then with layers of woven cloth and leather about their bodies
they faced the cold wind and sleet, set sail, said a prayer.
They did not come all at once
but little by little over five hundred years.
They reached as far west as they could
to touch that magic place in the center of the sea
and mount the great curve beyond which
they would never return.
Right in the middle of the ocean they began to shed,
ancestry and heritage
dropping from their shoulders
as termites drop their wings.
Now they were transformed,

born again, born free, truly who
they were meant to be.
And this time they would try
to get it right.

It happened that we were gathering shellfish

for the sweetness of the meat and small pearls they grow inside their opalescent shells as flowers grow their seeds. We ran into the waves unafraid, laughing, our faces shining with salt spray and sun; we pushed each other into the water, splashed the little ones and pretended to be fierce. Ocean gave us her precious life with broad sweeps of her hand; in the receding foam on white and gold sand, you could see her fingerprints. You were just a shape on the horizon, something new from where the sun emerges before it begins to lick the dew from our sweet potato vines and passion fruit. We were gathering shellfish and running into the waves, laughing and splashing the little ones. Carried over your heads, as you came closer, we could see thin sheets of transparent shell, sparkling in the sun and moving in and out of cloud shadows. We saw you standing and again when you came ashore in creaking canoes. One of you stepped into the shallow seawater and turned around, around again, then fell to one knee and lowered the head as if ashamed. We were gathering shellfish.

You all had so much hair and you had it everywhere! And your bleached skin was neither tattooed nor painted as if you came from nowhere, could name no country as your own. We smelled your stiff and stinking garments, felt their heaviness from sea, sweat, and a dozen rains. Even as we are on the sea in our boats, we slip into the water and out with ease, bare our skin to Grandfather Sun, and dry ourselves in the wind. We were born silver fish or tadpoles, and we are never far from the water that gives us life. We never thirst; we never go hungry. On the sea and on our island, we are always at home. We drink the rain that falls almost every day, nourish our bodies with fish and shellfish, an abundance of fruits, heal our cuts and swellings with kelp and other sea plants we gather as they twist like flat green serpents on the surface. We were gathering shellfish, splashing the little ones, when we saw you on the distant horizon.

You had been inside your boat for a very long time; you were much too pale, your weakness showed in the trembling of your knees, the shaking of your hands. You were too thin; even your cutting stiff clothing could not cover where your bones stuck out. We knew that you were hiding your dead and wondered what they had done. We were relieved to see you pray when you entered our nation, happy that you knew you would sleep well this night, pleased that you accepted our gifts of food and medicine with humble gratitude. We saw you honor our land that had relieved your relentless journey; you laid your offering on the sand and spoke aloud in a solemn voice. We could not understand your words, but we knew that you needed your moment and so we drew ourselves into the palmettos to gather rainwater from inside cupped flowers. We were gathering shellfish and laughing in the waves.

We have traveled to many islands ourselves and some have never returned. Many of our people went east across the ocean but we never saw them again. No matter where we went, we never saw others like you. You must have come a very long way. You will find our fruits delicious, our waters warm and gentle, our springs sweet, our swimming and flying relations good to eat, our people generous and patient. In time you will learn our speech and we will learn yours. We will trade with you for we see the exotic things you have brought and we are eager to see what more you might have. We will teach you the names for the plant people, the animal people, for the spirits of this place. When you fall we will give you medicine for your cuts and broken bones. When you have fever, we will bring you a special water to cool you and let you walk again. There are places where you can plant your crops and build your houses as you would have them; we are millions of people on these islands, but we will make room for you.

We saw no women among you but you will find our women to have pure hearts and sure hands; your children will follow the clans of their mothers but they will also know your ways. You will build your chickees close to the sea and allow the sun to darken your skin. Your children and your children's children will run into the surf, unafraid of deep water and of the creatures living there. We were gathering shellfish, unafraid, splashing the little ones, laughing.

The Itch: First Notice

There
    between the brown bubbling mud
    of an old woman's memory
    and the angry girl within
        lies the frightened moth
        huddled with fragile dusty wings
        and swollen face
            at the edge of any light
            no matter how hot, how cruel,
            no matter if it is suicide.

            I am looking for my People.
            As I find the names
            I write them down,
            encasing the letters between
            the pale blue lines of my ledger,
            then draw them in the margins,
            give them wings or hooves or horns,
            make bloodlines snake
            from one to another
            and wonder
            if the green eyes on paper
            know they can climb the pen
            and pierce my veins.

Another desert wind carried me to where
coal smoke has blackened home and hearth,
where the white moth was forced
into deep camouflage;
    there are people,
    too young to know

that wisdom emerges
from under the rocks,
          that beneath their very feet
          is all the future,
          in the moist underbelly
          of what is holy.

          This too
          is where I am from,
a white haze morning,
purple peaks that rise
beyond the Joshua trees.

The Itch: Second Notice

Grandmother Rachel, see what they did
to the perfect clay bowl? Disfigured it,
paled it, paralyzed it. What now? It is not enough
to listen for a whisper beneath my hearing—
you must put your arms around the whole of me
and bring my mouth to your breast;
you must turn me so the wind will twist my tongue
until my talking comes out right and the dust
is wiped from my eyes.
    Teach me what it means
    to be in the circle
    irrevocably, beautifully,
    impossibly
and I will teach you
how it feels
to be on the outside of outside
dissipating on the desert wind.
        Grandmother Henrietta, hear a Highland echo
        from the granite you sweep so furiously,
        raging at the dust and all the thousand eyes
        focused on your broom. Grandmother Sarah,
        you are so thin, always so thin;
        you sway with each breeze
        in Ontario snow, looking east,
        praying in a Protestant way
        for the thunder and mist of Niagara to part
        so you can remember
        Inverness.
Grandmother Margaret, leave the gun on the rack.
The sound that excites the chickens
and makes the horses stomp

is only your descendants
restless at the door. These
are not ghosts but flesh
tied to future, what you said
you would make,
after you rode the ocean
to the other side of the world.
We did not drown along the way,
not every dream, every wish,
so do not let us fade
from prophecy. And let
the evening rain fall.
Grandmothers, I know there are some
who carry their homes around on their backs.
Others just leave; still others pick up
what sticks and twine from the ground they find
and weave them together until they make sense
and the fingertips bleed. Some grow and shed
like king snake when he swells
beyond the bounds of bright skin;
some burst from the chrysalis fully formed
and crouch with their backs to the sun
so that moist wings slowly unfold and dry
in the four colors of creation.

    Others retreat
to the time before the morning of Emergence, the very day,
and hide behind clay as yet unformed,
or decide to stay, remember, transform.

O Elders of the world,
Red Gold Ebony Alabaster Elders,
tell the children the truth.
Tell them that if they give in

to the insatiable itch,
their roots will break open,
expose tender flesh
to blowing dust and searing heat,
may not set seed
in the crumbled dark earth
of other lands.

Genealogical Research

She carries a small pouch.
In this she puts the names,
nothing more. Collecting names
like pretty leaves in October
or shells swept into her hand
by the receding sea or picked
like peaches from a hardwood tree.
She collects the names.
Puts them into a pouch.
One hand shades her eyes
in case the sun should see
the glistening tear
that trembles and slides;
from the other hand hangs
the pouch filled with names.
　　She walks
　　in no particular direction.
　　One eye turns out, the other turns in;
　　so little to see of some names
　　as they fall or race away.
　　She holds the pouch closer,
　　tightens her grip.
Someone nuzzles her breast from long ago;
she strokes, murmurs, listens
for the sound of small bubbles
but it is only the pale spring rain
licking gray granite rock.
　　Names rattle at the bottom of the pouch
　　where bruises are kept blue, wounds
　　are held open. Here ghosts glow and seethe,

    pull one another

    maddened by jealousy.

Some names float to the top

no matter where the future should perch.

There is always someone to judge her,

how very light or very dark she is,

how fat or bony, how stumbling and lost,

how resolute or uncertain,

how very much or very little

she seems like them. They slip beneath

the surface again.

    How could they ask

    where she got the habit

    of rolling garnets

    around in her mouth,

    bringing them to her opening lips

    to where a magic light will touch them,

    set the embers on fire

    with the great power of secrets.

Sing her the prayer

    of home dissolving.

Sing her the seal

    for her pouch of names.

Sing her the way

    to a home on the moon.

Sing her dark disappearance

    from the soft flesh of earth.

Aborigine and Queen

If I were to go to the Queen of England,
curtsy, and say, Hello there! I am your cousin
from the colonies, the part you let go

till you started to dig beneath the moat,
then broadly smile from the center
of my round and brown face,

would she ask me to stay
for a spot of tea, sweet biscuits, nectarines?
Would she send me on tour to the Tower

where the crown jewels are jailed,
let me try on my hand a few emeralds,
diamonds, rubies, imperial war booty,

bracelets for my large bony wrist,
and place her captured gold crown
and all of her ancestors' ghosts

on this ancient and monstrous head?
And would I tell her then
the turquoise secret of sky,

show her inlaid shell from the Gulf,
the depth of earth's jet and mammoth bones
that ponderously walk from my father's dreams?

And would she answer
with the sparkle and gleam
of shared genes?

Would she dance me down the great hall
with confidence and grace,
the fancy old names surrounding her tongue,

waving an upright hand to larger-than-life portraits
one by one they come: Dunboyne, Massy, Plantagenet,
de Bohun, Stewart, Butler, de Beaumont, FitzGerald,

de Burgh, de Lacy, Campbell,
O'Brien, mac Murrough, and more
down the long mirrored hall of this passage
in which signs of myself are suspended
from one or another gilt picture frame,
square stance, short stature, mountains on my face,

round ripe melons of hip and thigh, anything whereby
the stranger would see first one then the other
and say, Ah yes,

she is certainly one of these.
O your majesty, old woman, grandmother,
the lie spills out from the gargoyle's mouth

and the castle is left unprotected.
I come as both the colonial thrust
and the native wound,

Old Britannia, I haunt you
building your face
from the blood of night air.

I am the mother of your soldiers,
your majesty, your grace,
the silver vein in the mine

the daughter of corn,
the soft salamander who lives
beneath the mossy stone.

I am the sun terribly undone,
mistress of many wars,
euthanasia at the end of time.

Turning

The song is Gaelic now,
peridot words
the color of fresh
timothy gathered
by red-haired women;
or the song
is the bony white oak
and rhythm of *Miwu,*
a knowing that breathes
against angles of granite
and meets the ground
in a flurry of sound.
Or the song rides down from a star
over burgundy boulders
beneath a dazzling blue sky
to find the old words
buried deep in the earth.

But this heart listens.
This song. *Hi-tsah-tsi-nah,*
the precious rain awakening.

On this you come
as a prayer in the flesh,
on this you ride
with the roll and rollick
of rattlesnake.
On this you sing
volcanic birthing words
and obsidian cools where
the blood bubbles down.

Oh look, a little girl is lost
although she stands close
to her mother's heart.
With great energy she scrapes
the missionaries from her ribs.
Shoulder blades curve
around the spine
and the pestle dances,
acorns flying,
and dust collects
in the creases
of her hands. Or

she is kneeling in a small room
at the edge of the mesa,
polished black bone of earth,
cherished *piki* stone,
moving back and forth
this act of love, grinding
the corn until it is dark,
brushing the white cornmeal
into one basket, the blue
into another, thinking already
of the daughters she will bear
glowing in the sun.

Or she is standing at the bog
inside a mountain meadow,
hands raised up to tie back her hair
with a thin red rag; seeds loosen
and cling to her shoes, her stockings,
her long skirt, her skin.
She fearlessly walks
through gold fiddleneck,

small mountain lupines, clouds
of white popcorn flowers fallen upward
out of the ground
to cover the hillside
like snow. Or

       a woman gathers loop after loop
       of heavy rope to guide the head
       of the horse she straddles and sometimes
       she is the mare and the soft sandstone
       and the hot rocks rolling in acorn soup,
       trying to heal the gash spread across her path
       where the crescent moon has sliced the earth.
       Ocean to mountain to mesa, the bundle she carries
       is a sacred memory, a rainbow that arches
       from one side of the sky to the other.

Or a woman is closing
a steamer trunk, has to sit on it hard
to get the latch through and
the leather buckled; seagulls dive
outside the wall of the ship, she
hears their demands, maybe one
has come inside to brush her cheek
with its pointed wing or maybe
just another tear warmed by cooling blood.

How she aches in the cold, she is so thin;
and when she pulls the blanket around her
and lies down on the floor, she is no more
than a pile of old rags, a few sticks of firewood,
a broken broom. Steady against the roll of the sea
she is patient as the rocks that wait for the ship
along a northern corridor, angry as the storms
midway across the Atlantic that shake their fists

at those who must leave home, and as deeply hidden
as the icebergs that threaten to disembowl.
She has already seen the world dissolve;
now she feels the breaking
of one last thread
to ancestral land,
feels the very break
of it.

Dear Grandfather Webb from England

How cruel
that when the babies
are thrown away
they do not die
but circle forever
in the evening news,
stories that hide,
a thirst that scurries
into the rain, a reflection
within your great looking glass,
little things with copper skin,
obsidian eyes, signs of the places
you colonized, unfinished murders,
incomplete demolitions, women
with furies half won,
hearts half broken,
the sticky birch leaf,
the wormy acorn,
blackberries that bristle
on a Berkeley back fence.
A girl runs the length
of the bay tree canyon
to find and carve some secret place
between the sweetly cured tobacco
in your favorite meerschaum pipe
and the pages you made into a prison
to trap and press the flowers you would find
in a book bound with leather,
girl with eyes dark as decay,
goes into forever, touches only
the rage of ghosts

with her skin of moonstone,
sits rocking and remembering
you not remembering her.

Margaret Castor

Born 1832, Darmstadt, Germany
Died 1925, San Francisco, California

The dangerous dreams
of a wild girl, they said,
who goes west
to meet her husband
beneath the twisting serpent
and eagle of Mexico's flag,
    who mounts the wagon
    bound for California
    where the very streets are gold,
    gold on which stolen kisses fall
    not gently at all
and the sun glimmers
from a thousand Spanish swords,
fire from the mouths of muskets,
and men ankle-deep already
in Miwok blood.
                Gold the river that pulled you west,
                the tall grass, vermilion poppies
                rising from rock and swamp;
                red the Missouri mud
                that transformed you
                at the border and this—
                that you might imagine me
                and all who come after.
        The rivers Merced and Mokelumne,
        San Joaquin and Fresno,
        feed great pastures, tules amid
        the streams of blood, secret shining crops

that moan and tremble at night, Bear Creek blood,
blood of Mariposa, Yosemite blood,
Ahwahneechee blood, places dark and toxic
from the rain of red water that will never end,
the blasting apart of the mountain's bones.
Emiliana, Elfriede, Lenchen,
pictures on brittle cardboard
of corseted girls with their tortoiseshell combs.
Did they watch you step onto the boat?
Dear friends, did they dream shut the sails
and will the wind to die?
Did you think of impaling yourself
on the pointed mouth of the ship
or of drowning yourself daintily
    in the lapping gray sea?
Did you give one glance back,
one final goodbye, words
    that must
    last a lifetime?

Into the muscle and flesh
of what you called wilderness
you drove the brown horses
through skinny jackpines
and crooked white oaks
ignoring the drought.
You brought to life
the anxious temblor
at the valley's edge,
both in the mountain
and in my heart
the shaking
has not stopped.

Are you the astonished one
or am I that we meet like this

between the sailing ship
and the silver jet
that crosses the sky?

More than a century later
my brown hands cannot recall
your Germany or your Mother Lode,
Yosemite untouched by tourists
and car exhaust, buying ice cream and souvenirs,
trying to pet the young deer in velvet,
or feed the bears by volition or by accident,
all of this along the broken back
of old Tenaya. How this question burns,
summons fire, conjures a younger sun
that never showed its face to Europe
and never will.

> If you are a part of me,
> I am that crazy acorn
> within your throat
> around which pioneer stories
> rattle and squirm.
> If you are the brave heritage
> of Gold Rush California,
> I am the bone that buzzes
> behind your breast.
> If I am the tongue made indigenous
> by all the men you would love,
> I am also the ghost
> of the pioneer's future.
>> Native storms wail,
>> and death rides through the frontier
>> switching sides continuously.
> I am the other voice
> blasted from the mountain

by hydraulic cannons,
the other fetus
embalmed on your knee.

Touching the silver
that has touched us both,
your emeralds and white lace,
my turquoise and seashell,
I believe you understand.
                    Do you remember
                    the sacred signs painted
                    in startling blue
                    on the backs of warriors,
                    spirits that mumbled
                    in the German Black Forest?
                    Do you remember the tribes
                    that so loved their land
                    before the roll
                    of Roman wheels?

Joseph Bigler

The cactus has its eyes on you
as you sway on the seat
of your hooded home,
rolling west on wood wheels,
strips of leather twined through your fingers,
the clacking of your tongue and a mild slap
of the reins onto the backs of the horses
who plod and snort through the mountain pass
and down the other side, crossing valleys,
the creek sometimes dry, sometimes fully in flood.
The horses and you, your ribs quiver
with hunger and pain; you worry about Margaret
but she holds her own and the babies are fat.
Someone shouts and I see you look up
and reach for the rifle beneath the seat.

    Great-great-grandmother Margaret,
    I see you too, peering from behind
    the veiled face of the wagon
    at what disappears
    along the ruts
    made by other wheels.
Without a word you move to the front,
the babes in their beds, and grip
the thin slatted seat; Joseph reins in the team
with a lurch.

        Don't stop, Joseph, don't be a fool.
        You camp too close to autumn's back.
        Press on. Winter will turn
        the birches brittle,
        and brown eggs grow already
        on the branches of buckeye.

Storms will soon swirl about your feet,
freeze your water, steal your breath,
mire your wheels in mud then hold them
until sun returns to melt the ice.
Prairie-dog holes and badger burrows
give way beneath the horses
who never knew they would walk so far
or pull a load so heavy. It seems
as if everything is falling
into the endless throat of the earth.

Then summer; trees leaf out
but the women and men you know
have turned hard.
The aching aspens whisper
to teach you prayers you can't hear
on this side of the ocean, drop seeds
on your shoulders, put burrs in your boots.
Rattlesnake shows herself to remind you
from which way the rain will come
and you shoot her golden head off,
never mind the luminous magic
or the future that hangs from her tongue.
Now the blanket is spread on the ground
and the babies walk unassisted.
Too late to get across before snow
so you seek the safety of mission or outpost,
remember a few words of Spanish
from the old days, a few new words in Navajo.
Out there, bent into the shape of an ancient cholla,
you will see a woman you do not know
but she has watched your every move
and it was she who led the horses
where you thought they would not go.

Margaret is in this cactus
but you cannot see her there.
    Remember the wagons you cannot drive,
    baskets full of seeds you can't eat,
    that a white man waits for you
    and sharpens his knife, cleans his gun,
    squints at the rising sun of Bear Valley.

    Cactus woman understands
    every atom of you.
        She fries with your meat
        and boils with your beans.
        The plains are flooded
        with her enormity
        and she bears the scars
        you will learn to love.
Shaking with rage, she knows you
the way madrone knows the smell
of your approaching axe.

Margaret Mourns the Death of Joseph Bigler

They tell me Joseph is gone.

        Just this morning
        he finished his gravied bread
        and thanked the good Lord
        for having it, an end to hardtack
        and jerked beef, the occasional fish,
        along the road.

Our horse was so thin,

        the wagon so filled
        with dust and then water,
        smell of mildew and rot,
        even our daughter's little feet
        turned black as the lava rock
        we see from time to time,
        as the earth through which
        we cut with our wheels.

O Joseph, these long long hours

        by candlelight;
        the careful plans gone
        with that extraordinary power
        in the aiming of the gun,
        gone with the singing
        of the bullet.

            I believe I will let
            the cabbage go to seed
            and the house needs
            new whitewashing.
            Tomatoes near ripe,
            all the small begging birds,
    the memories that sweep
    across the sawdusted dance floor

and my wedding dress cut
into tablecloths and curtains.
Oh, Joseph, what shall I do?
There is my little box of pictures
beginning to curve from winter's water
and then spring and summer and winter
again, bending up at the edges like wings.

        The fiddleneck has died back;
        cottonwood looking unkempt
        where the twigs are most tender
        and the leaves transparent; lupines
        and poppies disappear with the sun
        and the gray-needled bullpines loom

and break against
the stark white moon.

Exactly at the center
of the window in front
a woman stands alone
or she is
an outcropping
    of stone.

Margaret Opens the Bon Ton Saloon

BEAR VALLEY, CALIFORNIA, 1859

To let: solid building, two rooms, suitable for enterprise and hard work.
Frontier town on the Mariposa Grant at the south end of the gold-bearing
country. Local Indians pacified. —John C. Frémont, Owner*

I never liked that man.
My new husband, Maurice,**
thinks the world of him.
"John Frémont will be president one day,"
he says with a grand wave
of his soft Prussian hand
(grander than the wave he gives me
when I saddle the mare for a ride).
We would do well enough
to sell sarsaparilla and biscuits
but Maurice says no,
the miners must have
their Saturday spirits
and we will collect
their gold.

        There is not another white woman here.
                But I am strong.
        I listen without flinching
        to the cattlemen and miners
        explode through the door
        with the dust of the road

*Although the sale occurred as it is written, the ad itself is fictitious.
**It was always emphasized in my family that the name "Maurice" was to be pro-
nounced "in the English way," like "Morris."

settling on every surface.
(And sometimes the Indians
come round. The women
don't like me but the men,
the men are not so bad-looking
—for Indians, I mean . . .)

Let hang the next story writer
who comes to my table
with notebook and camera
to ask of my long memory
of the rocking on the northern sea
and slow bump of wagon wheels
in the endless tall grass prairie
giving way to sagebrush and stone,
cactus and high mountain passes,
blue lakes, deeply scarlet flowers,
a multitude of pigeons overhead.

I will not say I did not hunger
or that when the Indians came to the wagon
I did not fear (though it was only berries
they wanted to sell, berries for bullets
or buckets or steel knives) but I will say
San Francisco was sweet and the stage
to Mariposa smelled of the sweat of men
and cloying perfume from long petticoats
that would rustle in the scrub oak leaves
and sop the water from foothill creeks.

Castle Blake, Tipperary

Beg you beg you let me take
the turning of the year
into my redbud heart.
     I came in the mist
of your dream, the girl
gathering seeds.
     The gray granite peaks and I
spoke from the ground,
echo and motion beneath your feet
gone
     when you finally turned around
and my form rose from the ashes
of the old ghost camp
and shriveled black leaves
     of dry creosote.
          Here you come
          with your fortune
          though it barely kept
          your family fed
          and one day it was gone
          completely and just like that
you were helpless and shivering
at the castle door, farming not barley
but despair, hunger gathering, a cloud of vultures
over your wife and children.
All of them, yourself, and one old maid servant
who might have been your cousin,
to go and board the *Bolivar*
bound across the sea
and beyond that to Ontario.

You could not have known
the muttering ghost
who followed you
though you might have noticed
some motion and thought
just a mouse on the ship's floor
but when you turned
to put your eyes more fully upon it
nothing was there. Nor could you have known
there was not one ghost but two,
barely heard whispers in Gaelic, others in a language
so ancient you will never understand
the mountains of Mariposa
with their hundred tongues.

We watched you burn your roots on the beach
rolling the new and tender shoots
between the palms of your hands
until even you would spiral and weave
to the song of Spider Grandmother,
even you who abandoned your seeds
in the distant storms of Arizona.
                              We were with you in Canada
                              when you built your great house,
                              and named it for the elms
                              (that later died
                              from a kind of smallpox
                              they brought for trees).
Before Ontario
there was Sorel,
moss on stone steps,
loyalists like you,
and winter so quiet

you find yourself looking
for the world you once knew.
        Then come the dreams
       in which the severed limbs of infants
       ride river currents on split ash rafts
       and you remember how very far you are from home.

You do not name your ghosts
or the song you thought you heard
when timbers creaked in water and wind,
or a twig caught fire and cracked in the stove.
The ghosts of the unborn follow you
with life unraveling. Count every step
from Clonmel to Sorel,
from Sorel to Vittoria.
Every single step.
        Merced, California. 1985. Someone said,
        Whatever happened to Castle Blake? Judge Barrett
        said, "The Irish blew it up." Uncle Joe opened
        the slim envelope to show pictures around
        but later we heard he got it wrong; it was not Blake
        but the abbey ruins nearby.
        They graze dairy cows there,
        the fence, the farmer, the absence of signs
        a way to keep those out
        who would dismantle the memories
        stone by stone, knock down the tower,
        dig up the bones.

My camera never found the target
and I never touched the sea you crossed
except for the time I took the train from Boston
to the end of its line, an abandoned amusement park

across the road from the beach. Just so I could say
I have touched the two great oceans of Earth
I took my shoes off and stood
for just a minute or two
in an inch of glassy water
then retreated to land
to stand with Arthur looking east
over the stretch where you looked west.
    A block away there was a corner
    where the sign said "coffee shop:
    the pot is never empty" so
we went inside, sat down, waited,
just Arthur and me, a never-empty pot
we could not see. Finally he rose from the table
and asked someone for two cups of coffee
and some milk.
I am quite sure they speak English
in Massachusetts but she said
we have no coffee here. No coffee ever.
By that I knew, no matter what my feet had touched,
I could not leave the America you craved. Someday
you may go to your favorite tavern
and drink just enough
that from the corner of your eye
you will see brown-skinned women
roll their hips like dice
beyond your bedroom door.

    Cows graze the cracks
    where a parquet floor
    was polished and danced upon
    by Irish feet, where half the babies born
    never grew up, where other ghosts

compete for your attention
or attach themselves
to your soul like burrs.

Hugh Massey Barrett

Daughter, I slipped from Ireland
like a long sigh
          for there is thunder here
          or cannonfire, I cannot be sure,
          and also the sound of ancestry
          pulling loose to the laughter
          of the canny red fox who zigzagged
          before my father's horse and caused him
          to die at twenty-five.
          I remember the snap
             at the end of it all
and distant gray clouds on the horizon
where I wet my feet
in the aching Atlantic
even as the walls collapsed
around my bones.
          Castle or cottage,
          feudal lord or farmer,
          tacksman or baron,
          pauper or prince,
          all of them tumble
          together in my blood.

I leave them to you,
I leave this heritage
cracked and killed,
displayed with thread
pulled from thread,
comfort gone the way
of all murdered things.

Old Blake.
Stones huddled where they fell
on soft dark soil, picking them up
with moss beneath my nails—
it was the ship *Bolivar* or
the pistol for me.
 There are so many
 many mouths to feed

how could I not
burn up the roots
in a great pile
on the beach?

Thinking of Andrew in Orono, Maine

Soldier trees in their old red coats
guard the farms and the roads
where black bears huddle till spring
and blueberries dream of the day they will open.

April finds the Penobscot full
though redbud is bare
and birches still bend their antlers
over new-fallen snow.

Not far from this place
Andrew built "Aberfoyle"
from what was left
of a slaveowner's fortune.

In the tavern they called him "the laird,"
a title my mother took as fact
but I heard it repeated by mocking crows.

Upending his mug of ale
he may have laughed or sang
or maybe not, some old song
from home or told again
of when he went
on Grand Tour.

He may have strolled along the lake
remembering Loch Ness
where his daughter was born
or he may have straddled
a fine gray hunter or sat
upon a pretty carriage drawn

by matched hackneys or marched
with the Norfolk militia
to rage against the ones
who looked so much like me.

Pay attention, Andrew,
for this is as much memory
as prophecy.   Your daughter will seek
               the western edge of Turtle's Back,
               will mine for gold, will manage
               a dry goods store, and will marry
               a reckless prospector
               whose name will be Joe.
               Then she will wet the hem
               of her sweet petticoat
               in the surly ice melt
               of the Merced.

                              Some scars, Andrew,
                              are those we keep.
                              Others rise by themselves,
                              ripen like berries
                              on the backs of the beaten.
                              And there are those that howl
                              from the strangled throats of poets
                              freezing in the subway steam.
                              And some will take a spirit rifle
                              and shoot back, Andrew, shoot back.

Andrew MacInnes, You Look West
Just at the Moment I Look East

and the story will rumble from underground
of the words left unspoken, the names never heard,
Yoruba, Taino, Pict, Celt, or as all the villains do
you say, "Let bygones be bygones, get over it,
grow up, get with the program, let us say
nothing happened that way and if it did
it must have been your own fault."

Someone grows fat on your crimes, someone fails to grow;
smallpox, AIDS, poverty, the grinding truth I conjure,
Oh, yes, conjure, conjure the bygones, the red plantation
and its crop of blackened bones, Sky Woman falling
into your stomach with bygones engraved on the shell
of Turtle's Back, the loose strands of bygones twisting in the air
where Grandmother Spider has hung them
to harden in the dry desert wind of the future.

Your children will dance the bygones of you
for you rattle your veins like distant thunder
without the promise of rain. You are not quite a memory
nor are you a myth,

                    nor are you the clear cool brook
                    over rotting sycamore leaves,
                    or the blood that swirls
                    and mingles with fish.
Condor will teach them if you will not;
your grandchildren's grandchildren will know
how to crouch and howl like trapped wolves
so loud you will hear them beyond the grave.
They will pound their fists on the ground

and you will think you hear a million buffalo
running over the land. Your children, Andrew,
will go native, they will dance
to the rise and fall of summer,
surround winter's lodge
with their crackling song.

So bring to the table Taino and Mohawk,
Chukchansi and Hopi, Mandinka and Ibo,
Pict and Celt; pile up the ghosts
on autumn's cold ground;
gather acorns
where baskets are born.

Captain Andrew MacInnes of the Norfolk Militia

Oh feel the warm winds that kiss old Antigua
sending north and west the budding willows
and their awkward memories
of when they were burnt
by the rumbling heat of your passage;
feel the sea, turquoise tidepools
among black rocks and white sand,
curved bits of pale pink coral, hermit crabs,
fat anemones that loosen themselves
in the water then tighten at your touch;
cactus crossing the beach like serpents.
Feel your ivory fist beating on her breast,
on the earth, I mean, in a rage of male rain,
her song so secret you don't even know
you have missed the whispered words
and so even as I raise my face
to your blood that is my blood
I cannot capture what you mean
as you swim into my trap like a trout
and bump against the way out.

Where have I gone and what have I done
to find you? Stuffed the cracks in my heart
with tar and twisted the long lance into earth
with the strength of a ghost, seeking your bones,
sucking your dust. Andrew, I too am a ghost.
I come into your world and do the most dangerous
things although I was warned. I stupidly rushed
to your tomb and broke my fingernails
scraping for your name.

Great-great-grandfather, because you were
who you were, I must beg the islands for mercy.
Now I beg you to explain it all, the song
that swamps this ground with sludge, the song
that tugs at my hair for apology. Sparkling in the sky
red and black hands, thousands of backs that bear scars,
a million thin voices from the cold northern fog.
Know this. The first time I heard your name
I resurrected you to the place where I lived.
I made you in my image, imagined you as native man,
freedom fighter, resister of Brit domination, victim of Clearances,
wearer of tartan. I had it all figured out, looked it up
in a book under "MacInnes Clan." Rather than remain
in your Highland home, you put
your people first, took them to Canada
to wait for an end to genocide, waited
until cries of remorse would stretch west
across the Atlantic to the exiled clans.
In a symphony of cannonfire and blood
that sprayed your green tartan scarlet,
you fought for your land, for your people,
a warrior, the best of the best,
a man still at war with an alien force.
Ontario and its white pine woods would serve
to shelter the dream and the tartan turned camouflage
redbud, birch, blood on white snow.
Then you would wait the long weekends out,
the Scottish boulders in your bones growing larger,
the memory of what they did growing sharper.
You would stroll the lakeshore through purple heather,
as I walk the sunset orange of western poppies.
You would find and pluck a great thistle flower
to put in your cap as I might take the red-tailed hawk feather
dropped into the bowl of a grinding hole.

O but Andrew,
that was an image carved in wax
and with the rising of the sun
you tumbled into pieces.
You were one who bought other men
to work so you would grow rich
beyond measure; you stole them from their land,
their people, took their names, their languages,
turned them into blank slates upon which you would write
with the flick of your whip.
You did not resist British tyranny at all
but prided yourself on being loyal
to a throne your ancestors denounced.
You were not the noble Celt
with roots twisted into elaborate knots
beneath the cold surface of the Oban shore,
but the son of cattle thieves and outlaws
from another clan who changed their name
to avoid arrest. So it is with new knowledge
and half-blind eyes that I come to you
in my melon-round and earth-brown form,
to find you imagining me
to be as white as you, as petite
as your daughter, Henrietta,
the obedient girl
with flaming red curls.
I know your secret.
I know about the exiles, the thefts,
the selling of the clan name,
the patron who helped you (who fathered you?),
and the many spirits you tried to conquer
among Drummonds, Grahams, Swans, and Clarks.

What do I do with you, many-times grandfather?
Where do I put you? Do you enter my dream again?
Do I divide my own past into "before I knew" and
"after I knew"? Do I let your blood run back into my veins
or pinch them off in some desolate place
between Arizona and Ontario? Do I bring you west
to blue Hopi corn
and let you touch vermilion rock,
or take you past the mesas
to where thick acorn soup drips from my fingers
into your heart? When you open your mouth
do you speak to me? Or does the wind rush about
hopelessly mute? Here—yerba santa from the Sierras
to renew your voice. Here—steps carved into the granite
for you to climb following me. Here—the white horns
of jimsonweed, small fat peyote on the ground,
a harvest of toads. Does this make you forget
who you are?   Here—a mask to paint
as white or red as you like, or the two crossing
as in a plaid—black oak leaves
attached like banners to the bottom of your boot.

Henrietta's Song for Joseph

In Canada
      I could wear his hands
      of speckled red, like ribbons
      about my neck or curled
in my crop of strawberry hair
      the camera caught so well
      when we rode
      to Merced that cool November day
and stopped for our pictures.
      Now see him as he hitches the horse,
      hands heavy and coarse with scars,
      callouses formed from the rub of reins
      and the scrub of sorghum from
      the dry goods counter
or the trigger he lays his finger upon
      when the miners come in from the field.
      I tell him—take care of your gold,
      wisely invest, not in this
      godforsaken place
      but where decent folk stay,
      San Francisco or Monterey,
      some pretty place with beaches
      where black shadows unfold,
      Spanish lace across gold sand,
      and the cypress kneels
      twisted by incessant wind.
He loves that river
      with its narrow crossings and ice water,
      these oaks that drop their leaves in winter,
      the thin gray pines, the bitter and brittle
      berries of fall.

He tells me—stop worrying so much. Don't cry
　　for the babies buried in Ontario snow.
　　Do not lie awake remembering
　　that you held them for such a short time;
　　we will have more. But, I tell him,
I would be more comfortable
　　if summer did not run our sweat into streams
　　deeper than his river, lonelier than the full moon
　　of August and the smell of smoke, the sound
　　of a thousand cicadas.

Joseph

Born 1824, Castle Blake, Tipperary, Ireland
Died 1904, Merced Falls, California

Emerging from between the reeds
a long-legged white egret steps,
dips for waterbugs and crayfish
with his ivory spear; bone-hard feet
pick their way among the tules
and white silk trails in still water
from that great pointed mouth.

Or just an old man
leaning into his wire-and-spindle chair,
forelegs off the weathered floor
of the peeling blue porch
and its woven willow roof.
Along the top of the chair, his arms,
white sleeping serpents, patches of pink
and white whiter than white, red down backlit
by early morning sun.
        Tough old miner,
keen eye for the quartz that bears
gold or sometimes pyrite,
greenbacks that flash back and forth,
over and under, across and around
the counter.
                Old miner, old gambler,
                who went for the Big One,
                California, 1849, only one year
                a reluctant part of the United States,
                tough old man who gained and lost

a dozen fortunes, killer
who turned his weapons upon
his own delicate mother,
the red earth of home
and its white-veined granite,
reshaping her flesh
with hydraulic cannons,
causing great injury to bone and soul.

Or the boy who complained
of cracking open boiled eggs
packed in sawdust and flour
on board the *Bolivar* in 1830
and later said he'd rather starve
than eat another pancake so tough;
boy who felt the Atlantic rise and fall,
did not recognize in the rhythm of his lungs
the breathing of ocean and moon.
Day after day, all those long nights,
and the horizon never changed,
so hungry and nothing to do but wonder
and dream
of mountains that rise
like blue whales from the plain,
lakes with the facets of precious gems . . .
For what does a twelve-year-old know of Transformation?
Does he fear the wilderness or does he taste it?
Does he face with British pride a fierce native warrior,
or think of dancing with young ladies
who wait in distant Sorel?
Winter mirage gives us Northern Lights,
blue streaks of cold fire
from where your new sun sets.

Great-great-grandfather Joseph,
of all the old bones of earth you broke,
what small bits did you keep?
What ground's blood covered your hands?
What metal screams were heard
when you opened the veins of the land?
       You tell me, thinking I am not there,
       bullets whisper past in the night;
       the oak leaves dance, brown and sharp
       on freezing ground.
Do you know the many names
of the one who opened
her wounds for you?
Do you know the voice
that sings beneath
the summer song
of obsidian crickets?
Do you know the bodies
that bubble from the ground
before their time,
touch and wrestle
the soaproot stalks,
and bend the spotted lilies back
to dig among their damaged roots?

      Look back, look ahead.
Do you see her? That woman
seated between shovel and pick,
her eyes as brown as October buckeye,
her hair a mass of tangled peat? Look close
and pull aside the old burnished doe hide;
see her memories and dreams.
Or tumble back to Ireland,

to the old Norman tower,
to the walls fifteen feet thick,
to where other women dreamed
and waited, shaking, for each babe to be born.

But you think your bombed and blasted mountain,
your bags of gold and silver, will keep you
from the fire. You know they will not.
I dream you better
than you dream me.
You balance from one broken rib
to the other on my back
and you become the secret pain,
the mystery in my bones.

Spring rains have gone crazy this way;
south wind is inconsolable.

The bruises and cuts fade from me as I sing.
They are rising on you, they are rising on you.

Defending Earth against the Gold Rush

(For Jesse, my daughter, who was almost born)

I will tattoo my face
with great nations
on the rolling brown
sea of me,
narrow lines and broad,
lightning signs and stars,
a badger, the sun, a planet
with a ring, comets that radiate
and shout to be closer
to the earth. I will make my bones
short and heavy, touch the lowest place
in the hemisphere, bless the small spears
of piñon taking root between my toes.
I will weather the year
good as any old rock,
lie down in the water
and be polished
by the first river
to surge down the mountain
when spring sun brings
the melted snow.
I will be less substantial
or more so,
an old thundercloud
with my fists raised over my head,
my feet falling hard upon the shoulders
of they who would turn the storm away;
I will return in night fog, remain as dew.
I will sing louder

than I ever sang before,
make a lot of noise,
make everyone turn around to see.
I will be a thousand young throats
purified by this new day;
I will be fat
        so very fat
the whiteman will find me ugly
and leave the old mountain
alone.

My Ghost Comes to Joseph Evans and Isabel Graham

I can hardly see you, woman.
You came for me? What the hell
do you want? Some people,
they'll say anything. Me?
I just followed the coal seams,
you know, all around the earth,
around the whole world.
Mined it in Wales, breathed it,
shoveled load after load
to feed the engine
across the ocean.
Ended up in Kentucky
where coal seams cross,
cross back. Got no schooling,
can't read a word. But
if you can't trust a man's *word,*
what's a piece of paper
going to do?

                You ask what made me leave.
                Was it the smoke, the danger,
                drops of blood on the coal
                like red-winged blackbirds
                nesting on the ground. Was
                it the explosions, the cave-ins?
                Was it how you could just
                drop dead for no reason at all
                and never see it coming?

    It was Isabel.
I met her in Missouri,
Isabel with the coal-black hair,
Isabel with dark seams crossing,

crossing back in her eyes.
Isabel in my blood, in my bed,
it was Isabel made me leave.
Digging, drilling,
beneath and above the ground,
darkness to darkness—
but Isabel had skin of velvet
the color of sunset in smoke.
Owned horses, too.

         So I got a hammer, old pine wood, nails.
         Made a wagon; had to buy the seat.
         Dried meat, made pouches for flour,
       sacks for barley, feed for the horses
       and livestock 'long the way.

The road from Grand Island was well worn;
you try to keep on level ground
but the ruts were deep.
Brought water, eggs packed in flour.
Our eyes burned in the afternoon sun,
the mornings burned our backs.
We reined the horses in, unhitched them.
I was the one who worried,
I was the one who doubted.
But Isabel said
     with her coal-black hair
     and shining deep eyes
I have a stallion
I have a mare
we will make do.

One-Way Conversations: Grandmothers,

I wake
with all your faces
as one with a coma
looking up
at the disembodied.
I roll down
the aching old hips
of the mountain,
dive just as
the glistening black beetle
taught me
at the beginning of time,
and bubble
above your cooking fire.
I unravel into the sandy grit,
long hair combed
in the wash
between mesas.   .
O Grandmother,
       I get it so mixed up.
       I wake to be the mop
       on broken linoleum,
       among potato peels
       and melon rinds;
       I am tossed
       for chickens to find.
       I am the red mare
       saddled for a ride or
       I am the saddle or the rider
       or just the idea of it.
       I am the roundup you rode

like any man, they said,
and I am your eyes,
pale against a parchment skin,
admiring the bullriders
at the rodeo.
I am the machines you feared,
the car you never believed
you could learn to drive,
the forty-niner in the goldfield,
forty-niner at the powwow,
the knee that is bent
in incessant prayer,
and the gentle fall
of Sierra snow.

Grandmothers, teach me
to do this better. Teach me
the bundle tied on your back
and the dance you do in the dark.
Teach me the worms, the flicker
of the moth, the acorn that falls
from your great burden basket.
Teach me eruption and running,
polished obsidian and jimsonweed
crouched by the side of the road,
teach me all the rocks.
Teach me red, teach me black,
the bitterness to be leached
from the buckeye with rain,
the little brown bead
that fell and rolled
underfoot, unseen.

1830 as I Remember It

I come
from where the living
haunt the dead.
We scrambled from our holes
like spiders, apparitions you saw
on the face of Mother Corn
or the boulder
where lightning strikes
before it jumps from there
to here over the mountain.
Wandering amid noise and names,
ancestors, would-be ancestors, the sun
that glistens on a thousand memories
from the wound where words come from,
or that other place
in its afternoon gray,
the surprise and glory
of the most ordinary.

Where are you, my grandmothers?
O mother of Kuyingwu
whose name should be
resting on my tongue.
O Clan Mothers, granddaughters,
all those the missionaries erased—
this is as it never was
and now even the bones
cannot call you back.
Where are you, Grandmothers?
What was given to me,
no more than fragments

of yellowed paper
crossed by faded blue lines,
curving and graceful letters,
anonymous postcards, a single envelope
with the MacInnes Clan crest,
and most recently, accounts
of how hard it was to sell eggs
on the outskirts of Santa Monica
in the years before World War I.
There are confessions from the perilous journey
that chemicals are disguises
to separate the hearts of gold
from surrounding stone
         and O this is why
                my bones hurt so!

Henrietta sails the sky,
navigates meteors and comets;
I know her by the soft red hair
backlit on the top of my arm
by summer's setting sun.
         Margaret, I feel your grip
on sea currents, suitcases, wagon wheels and reins,
babies, the blue ghost of hunger. And you
lived the longest of them all.
         Grandmother who is the acorn grinder,
the basket weaver, I know your ecstasy
watching dust devils on another hot day;
you are the scars on my thighs
that never fade.
         Grandmothers, sisters, will you look for me?
In the waking stretch of soaproot, the pollen on my face
and burrs carried about my ankles, the ochre quarry

of my veins. Know that they stopped the ceremony
with Spanish swords but you were the prayer
I ran to, you were the sun slipping away,
the twisted spine of the day.

PART TWO
This Heart

One of those days when I see Columbus

in the eyes of nearly everyone
and making the deal resides
in the touch of every hand.
                    Voices beyond
                    my office door
                    speak of surveys
                    and destruction,
selling the natives to live among strangers
to pay for the trouble of transporting them,
or mastering this or that, perceiving entitlement
good as gold for service
or kinship to the Crown.

                         Terror
                         crouches
                         in the canyon my hands make
                         and in the pink open rosebud
                         of the newborn; fear
                         rides the helpless old bulls
                         and the only songs
                         are ones ghosts sing.
Hispaniola. Sand Creek. Piedras.
Wounded Knee. My Lai. Acteal. My mother.
Gold-lichened boulders of Lilley Mountain,
grinding holes at the edge of the river,
channels where water has surged
to the rhythm of a collective heart,
to rise where refugees have stepped
deep in the mud on Turtle's Back . . . so

we choose our battles
and take our victories
where we find them:
                a sunflower refuses
                dormancy beneath
                the long deadly trail
                of a San Antonio sidewalk;
                spurge breaks through
                the smallest of cracks
                to erupt in fractal glory
                with secret milk it hides in its leaves;
                small twisted bits of placenta
                do not sleep
                but follow you
                around the world,
                emerging.

So dance the mission revolts,
let ambush blossom in your lungs,
claim the enemy's finest night,
sing, oh sing him to death,
for when he sees how strong
is spine tied to spine,
                woman holding woman,
Coyote will creep most quietly beneath
the ancient gallows that creak and creak . . .
                . . . must lure the soldiers
        into the trap,
must feed them
                dried mushrooms,
        old meat. . . .

International Hour of Prayer for the Yellowstone Buffalo Herd

Noon, March 6, 1997

From morning's mouth
the bones emerge,
a prayer is whispered
over rounded horns;
the prairie is beyond
the quivering hump
and holy smoke sparkles
released in the breath.
Braided sweetgrass,
be about their hooves;
although the grip of hunger
lies heavy on the land,
let endless native grasses grow
among the yellow stones
and between the stars.
Even if only one man had
begun to sing, actually
it was thousands, She who came
to Wisconsin farmers
and transformed their lives,
She who brought her blessing
in the form of being newborn,
She whom they named the Miracle,
White Buffalo Calf Maiden must return
amid the fast firing of bullets, along
the most perilous of paths. Rock stars,
millionaires, they all offered millions of dollars
to struggling white farmers
but she had begun her transformation and her prophecy

by touching them and they came to understand
if not the actual words to the prayers
at least the reverence, the need
to protect, to keep the doors open.
Like it was a hundred years ago
bounties are gathered from death;
trains, buses, cars, planes
carry the segmented body of the terrible worm
across the land and the screams of the hunted
split the sun awake. It is time to restore
the stolen beads and shards,
the bones and knives to every grave.
And the graves are graves no longer but wombs;
the bounties burn their hands
and bones come flowing
from museum shelves
to dance in the rippling grass,
rebuilding lungs, starting hearts.

             There must be a hundred men
             and a hundred men's worth
             of heartlessness; wished they could find
             Indians to kill but now that is illegal
             so they make up some excuse
             to raise their rifles and take aim,
             not hearing the rumble
             of buffalo prayer, not feeling
             tomorrow tremble
             or the prophecy of Miracle,
             and smile as they see the legs give way,
             the horns gouge open the prairie ground,
             Earth betrayed again.

I make this woman

of cornmeal and salt,
release her to morning
with the surprise of birth.

I loosen her grip
but she trembles in the clouds
with the seeds of life

under her fingernails. I set her on fire
and she smolders, sets opals down her cheek
and I open her eyes with my thumb.

I give her a sleep that will never rest
and let the embers glow relentlessly.
I pull her every which way, all through time.

I make this old woman
from the elements of rage
and rattle the earth with her hunger.

I make this woman from thirst
and break her open like a geode
eating her flesh like any old rock.

I shape her long and crooked, cold and hard;
I make her joints ache, her tongue complain,
her feet swell till she can't wear her shoes.

I make this woman
from years of blood
mixed with sand,
fallen on rocks.

Foremothers, I am that child

who breathed a name into your ear
on a mid-spring Saturday in the hope
you would remember and say it
when I emerged to live among you.
         You saw me coming
as on the high strong western wind
from within the great bowl
of your body and I see you searching
for what is missing and here I am
jumping up and down, waving my arms,
calling over and over, here I am!
Don't you see me? Can't you hear me?
I am the tear that dropped
from Moon's ancient face.
Look. I am the soot
on sparkling silver,
boots that crunch
the small toads. I am unexpected,
and I am the burning you feel.
I am the flicker of a shadow,
the crackle of the hearth.
I will arrange twigs and leaves
for my cradle just as I sing my own songs
to bring soothing sleep.

I rock back and forth imagining the gentle hand;
so place a small slow ember
on the small of my back;
it will mold to the shape
of my spine, elongate and slide
to make me one of you.

Build me from coils of river mud,
smooth my skin with a polishing stone.
East, west, over one sea or another,
I don't care, just tell me
welcome
welcome
be at peace
you can stay here.

Listen. This is the Lie They Believed

that the ravaged past may be let to drop
from the heart like so many rags,
that language may be stolen like money
and stumble through the echo
of a lingering sound, that our bodies
may be crushed to fit
the boundaries of appetite,
that the metal scream of bone wrenched from bone
would make this new thing, this america, this embryo
falling from the womb, refusing to see what embers
it spilled from the thousand fires it made.
And what of those tortured memories,
the weapon so carefully sharpened;
what of Mother who melted before them
so that soldiers would carry her treasured secrets
on their guns and saddles; what of the daughter
who explodes in the impact of asteroid,
nova of sun, relentless grind of glacier.

O tumbleweed,
you are so very far
from home.

Grandmother Rattler

who coils in my bones,
what were you thinking
that summer night
when you found the warm road
on the edge of the canyon
and stopped just there
exactly at the center
where the pickups and cars
and evening walkers would see
your spiral upon spiral,
hear the singing voice
of your tail,
see your black head
rising?

When I stopped my car
and walked up to you,
arms spread and hands open,
why didn't you move?
Why didn't you slide down the stones
among the white oaks
and single tall stems
of soaproot?

When those white people stopped,
leaned out of their truck,
whistled and hooted,
did you not recognize Owl among them
calling to me over and over,
"Kill it! Kill it!"   I would not, of course,
but still you would not move

even to save your life
but sang all the louder,
your body quaking
with rage.

Then the woman came out
of her house just there,
saw you, ran back,
picked up the heaviest shovel
she could find, pushed her way past
where I tried to shield you,
and said she would kill you
if I would not,
said she had horses down the hill
that might get bit, or she might die
if you were allowed
to live out the night.

O Grandmother.
What did I become?
The German mother who closed her ears
to the sound of neighbors
as they choked and burned?
Uniformed boy in a silver room,
his finger hovering over one small button
to kill thousands he will never see,
elders and infants he will only know
by the magic devil word "enemy"?
I know only this.
I took the shovel
wanting to spare you a death
at their hands, brought it down edgewise
on your soft red neck, cleanly sliced

the head from the body,
felt a shadow pass
over my womb.

Ever since
there is a dream
where opals outline
the shape of diamonds
on my back.
My mouth opens
and your high
whistling hum
bleeds out;
my tongue
licks the air.

Pahana Names the Mountain Flowers

This
I will do.
Grandmother,
begin to let fall
this alien blanket.
The seedheads,
the taproots,
white dusty leaves,
I will pull them out
one by one,
take from you this burden
and place my arms
around your neck
with four circles
of freshwater mussel
and white clam shell beads.
I will sing in your ear
the long low curve
of jimsonweed flowers,
keep magic charms
in green steatite
and shaped bits
of pink coral
that capture
this lethal rainbow light
where oil is on the water.
I will coil the serpent
about your feet,
at your wrist
tie soft red fur
of shredded cedar bark,

hide among the heads
of tall summer tules
that dance among your veins.
I will twine you a skirt
of condor wings,
weave the orange and black bands
of flicker feathers for your forehead.
I will moisten your skin
with your old lover mist
who whirls about the valley
turning to steam in late afternoon.
I will sew strips of rabbit fur
to wrap around your legs,
lick your wounds
where barbed wire runs,
fan the blisters
until they heal.
I will enlarge my mouth
and cover you,
absorbing the blood,
spitting it out
to root in this
aboriginal soil.
I will fill what is empty,
smooth what is rough,
call you by the thousand names
Pahana does not know.
And when I am done
I will dance with you,
eagle-bone whistle
between my teeth,
clapper marking
incessant strong beat
of your heart

and the bony scrape
of stone against stone
as acorns are ground.
Manzanita rises
like morning
under my navel.

Women Like Me

making promises they can't keep.
For you, Grandmother, I said I would pull
each invading burr and thistle from your skin,
cut out the dizzy brittle eucalypt,
take from the ground the dark oily poison—
all to restore you happy and proud,
the whole of you transformed
and bursting into tomorrow.
　　　　But where do I cut first?
Where should I begin to pull?
Should it be the Russian thistle
down the hill where backhoes
have bitten? Or African senecio
or tumbleweed bouncing
above the wind? Or the middle finger
of my right hand? Or my left eye
or the other one? Or a slice
from the small of my back, a slab of fat
from my thigh? I am broken
as much as any native ground,
my roots tap a thousand migrations.
My daughters were never born, I am
as much the invader as the native,
as much the last day of life as the first.
I presumed you to be as bitter as me,
to tremble and rage against alien weight.
Who should blossom? Who receive pollen?
Who should be rooted, who pruned,
who watered, who picked?
Should I feed the white-faced cattle
who wait for the death train to come

or comb the wild seeds from their tails?
Who should return across the sea
or the Bering Strait or the world before this one
or the Mother Ground? Who should go screaming
to some other planet, burn up or melt
in a distant sun? Who should be healed
and who hurt? Who should dry
under summer's white sky, who should shrivel
at the first sign of drought? Who should be remembered?
Who should be the sterile chimera of earth and of another place,
alien with a native face,
native with an alien face?

Signs of Survival: My Sister Weeds

There is one
who gives nothing away.
She lies down
with limbs stretched
to the four directions,
her face raised up
immense and bright,
a green spider dancing
for the sun on long days that linger
near summer's end.
It is her way that the flower never opens.
She only shows her gold petal tips
tightly bound at the end of a stalk,
red ants walk straight up and inside,
then outside and down, each with a pearl.
Some time before the sun comes up
she snaps open with a shout,
entire life span in a single moment,
gold petals become her crazy white hair.
Bending and letting the wind take her
she laughs out loud
at we who wait and demand
that a flower open completely,
without pretense or humor
or secrets that itch
and burst overnight.

          Grandmother
          for every bit of moisture,
             abundant
             life.

For every invader's footstep,
    a native
    soul.
For every one who prays and waits,
    a quiet,
    quiet hush.

Buckeye as You Are
September 11, 2001

They walk past you
                    weeping
                    for the leaves that burnt
                    & fell, the wood exposed
                    like bone, sculpture
               that suddenly emerges
               from white haze.
You old fortune-teller,
you could have told them
in their vibrant grief
whispering through the night wind
your breath held in your heart
like the trembling promise of tomorrow,
just before dawn
               there was no pain,
                    you are the wood
                         not the leaf,
                              falling is not
                                   falling but
                                        offering.

Scientists said they expect to discover space warps

"Within the next three years . . . new dimensions that have the potential to help scientists develop a theory that unites all the forces of the universe under one master explanation . . . the way we think about things is about to change completely."—Maria Spiropulu, quoted in United Press International wire release by Charles Choi dated Feb. 17, 2002

Her body is warm
you are sleepy in Her arms
that is all I can tell you

except for the way
She weaves and weaves
keeps us alive in mystery
in love   knowing there will come a day
when the weaving is finished
and the pattern is complete.

It takes eight hands to weave so much,
eight hands it takes
no matter where you go—
you find Her warp, you find Her colors,
you find a piece of the pattern She

                      is weaving.
            You have discovered
            nothing.

        Cobwebs in the corner,
        a rainbow of dew
        frozen on an orb,
        Her chalcedony belly
        at the center.

Epilogue: Leonid Shower, Late Fall, 2001
from the top of Lilley Mountain
looking east above the Sierra crest
and snow

      you have nothing left but your words
      & they tumble around
      in your hands like dice.
      Even the coffee
      is clumsy in its cup
      swirling to the brim
      & onto your knee.
           You stayed up
                so you
                  would not miss Her,
           She Who falls from the Sky,
           She Who sends the stars before her
           cascading like flowers or flowers that cascade
           like stars.
The volcano beneath your feet stirs
& it is the memory
      of when Turtle rose like lava
      expanding everywhere to touch everyone,
      after waiting so long
                asleep down below.
The shell of the egg
must actually crack,
the membrane break;
the seed must be bathed
in an acid bath, freeze,
thaw, freeze, thaw;
life always returns like that—
the fetus emerging wet & hungry,

first leaves more tender than air,
aimless fists that reach for the sun
remembering stars that fell to earth
& how life was only the breath held
until She could release the seeds
from beneath Her fingernails.
                    Now look
                    how silly all the words are.

PART THREE

Listen Here for the Voices

Much of the impetus to write this book is more personal than political. I had to come to terms not only with the obvious historical facts of conquest and genocide, but with the personal fact of being born into a family that could not keep its own secrets straight. The world was blue one day, red the next, then yellow. Nothing ever stayed the same from one telling of a family story to the next. My mother has even been known to contradict herself in the middle of a single conversation, and yet, on one occasion, she stood up to her aunt and defended the fact that I was Indian. Of course, my mother was also cheated out of any joy she might have felt in being "exotic" in largely white Berkeley; it was beaten out of her. It was not a good thing to be mixed; you had to be one thing or another. You had to be on one side of the fence or the other. You had to be of your mother's people or your father's people or maybe just the person who looked back at you when you looked into a mirror. This condition is a part of the "itch" that is growing in intensity as young people find themselves feeling alone because they are "multiracial," when in fact the majority of Americans will be multiracial one day in the near future. Alone in a crowd. The people who are the muscle and bone of the world and yet have been made to feel they are homeless. Our Elders tell us, no matter from which tradition they speak, that we come from Earth, that the substance of our bodies is the same as Earth and all living things, that our spirits are the same as Earth spirit—are parts of it. Scientists believe that they are pretty smart, but only now are they beginning to understand that all they really had to do was talk to the Holy People. And the Holy People are everywhere—all you have to do is see them and listen. That's why silent places are so important—the knowledge pumps in our hearts, and if it is quiet enough we can even hear and feel the electricity in our brains. The day came when it no longer mattered to me who my father was, Dick Edwards or Charles Loloma—it was too difficult, too depressing, too complicated to keep on trying to figure out this tangle of families who are always disguising themselves as something else. So I began to listen for the electrons and the heartbeat instead.

Madonna. My grandmother Clair Newman is gazing at my mother, Betty, in this beautiful Victorian scene, 1912. Her husband, my grandfather from England, Sidney Valdez Webb, was an art photographer who established his studio in Berkeley, California, sometime before 1910, the year of their marriage. Before finding his niche in photography, he tried his hand at chicken farming to sell eggs in Santa Monica, in southern California. This romantic madonna with my very young mother would have been photographed in their house or studio in Berkeley.

Generations Together. In the center, Henrietta MacInnes, my great-great-grandmother (wife of the 49er Joseph Barrett); she was born in 1832 in Fort Augustus on the shore of Loch Ness. On the left, Henrietta's daughter Mary Elizabeth Barrett, my great-grandmother (wife of Maurice Newman Jr.), born in 1859 in Merced Falls, California, on the Mariposa Land Grant of John C. Frémont. On the right, Mary's daughter Clair Newman, the grandmother I called "Nana" (wife of Sidney Valdez Webb), born in Mariposa, California, who daringly migrated to Berkeley before 1910. And the baby, of course, is my mother, Betty Webb, born in Berkeley in 1912.

Caroline Butler and Hugh Massey Barrett, my great-great-great-grandparents. Caroline Butler was born in 1793 in Kilkenny, Ireland. Through her relationship to the Ormond Butler family, she was eighteen generations removed from King Edward I of England and Eleanor of Castile. Caroline Butler died in 1874 in Toronto, Ontario. Her husband, Hugh Massey Barrett, was also her first cousin, through the Massy sisters, daughters of Lord Hugh Massy of Duntrileague in Limerick, Ireland, and his second wife, Rebecca Delap. Hugh Massey Barrett uprooted his family and brought them to North America in 1830 on a ship called the *Bolivar*. He was born in 1791 in Tipperary and died in 1868 in Port Rowan, Ontario. For reasons that no one seems to be able to explain, Hugh changed the spelling of the name "Massy" to "Massey" and his descendants maintain the new spelling.

Henrietta MacInnes. My great-great-grandmother Henrietta as a young woman. Her father's story is an interesting one, although one that is difficult for me to tell because much of it involves the anguish and terror that many of our ancestors felt, as well as people they never knew in this world who could, perhaps, share their suffering. My great-great-great-grandfather Captain Andrew MacInnes was raised by Sir Walter Scott (who was actually awarded guardianship of him) and educated by him at Peebles. He became a planter in the British West Indies on an island called Carriacou, and he was the last to comply with Great Britain's new law to abolish slavery. He migrated to Canada in 1840 and became a captain in the Norfolk militia of Ontario, presumably to fight the Native people. One of his sons was given the duty of guarding Tatanka Iyotanka (Sitting Bull) during his brief exile in Canada. I hope they shared a few good jokes and played cards. I recently contacted distant relatives descended from him who still live in Ontario; they always wondered what had happened to Henrietta. Well, she followed her forty-niner to California.

Family. A study in contrasts in Berkeley, California,
1912. How little my mother, Betty, resembles her
father and mother. Sidney Valdez Webb, my cold
and distant grandfather, was born in London in
1876. Supposedly he was German, English, and
Scottish, but new information is showing a strong
possibility that he was Scottish on his mother's side
(specifically the Campbell Clan of Glenfalloch) and
Jewish on his father's side. This is a conjecture, but
the more I discover about him in my research, the
more mysterious his family becomes. During the
time when all records in the family say that his
family was in England, the English census does not
record even one of them, much less the entire
family. The only record of any of them involved a
marriage of my grandfather's aunt that took place in
the Jewish Quarter of London, Whitechapel, which
was also famous for being the area where Jack the
Ripper committed his murders. My grandfather
married my grandmother Clair Newman in 1910;
she was a mountain girl from the southern part of
the Gold Rush country in California. If her husband
was a Jew, the irony would be complete as she was
vehemently anti-Semitic. Their baby and firstborn
child, my mother, was a bouncing, brown-eyed
Indian cherub who, in almost every picture taken of
her as a child, looked sad and solemn.

My mother, Betty Webb, with Duchess, our collie.
When I think of my mother, I think of her looking
like this even though I would have been about six
years old when the photo was taken. I fondly
remember Duchess, who lived into my teen years.
The picture was taken on a beach in northern
California or Oregon about 1954. My mother's
husband, Dick Edwards, took over his father-in-
law's photography studio and became a portrait
photographer as well. My mother took up art
photography and entered her work in photography
salons held in Berkeley at the little park where her
parents first met.

Margaret Castor, my great-great-grandmother. In early versions of the long poem about Margaret, she was called Margaret Newman because I had been told it was her name and that it was just a coincidence that she had married a man whose name was also Newman. It turned out that her family name was Castor, and so I hope no one gets too confused by the correction in the title of the poem. Her husband, Maurice Newman, was a Prussian draft dodger. He became her second husband after she had been widowed in Mariposa, California, and had "fraternized with the Natives." The son born as a result was named Maurice Jr., despite the fact that he was half Miwok, to make it appear as if he was the son of her new husband. She and her first husband, Joseph Buerckbuechler (anglicized to Bigler), had founded the Bon Ton Saloon in Bear Valley, California, at the southern end of the Gold Rush country during the 1850s, and Joseph had been shot in some kind of barroom altercation. They bought their house from John C. Frémont. Margaret was born in 1832 in Germany and died in 1925 in San Francisco at the home of her daughter, Emily Newman, who apparently never married. I wish that I knew more about the Miwok man that Margaret had known; Miwok people today in the Mariposa area tell me that they have heard stories about the Newmans and their own people, but no one can tell me the name or the clan of my biological great-great-grandfather.

Pauline Evans, my grandmother if Dick Edwards turns out to be my father rather than Charles Loloma. In practical terms, she was my grandmother anyway, as I never knew Charles's parents. Pauline was born in 1894 in Maxwell, California, in the Sacramento Valley. Her father was a horse breeder from Madeline Plain near the famous lava beds of Lassen County, and her mother, Minnie Bell, was part of a group of Native people in Chico. Everyone, including Pauline, just called them "Bidwell's Indians." I am not clear about which tribe they were or if they were a mixture of several groups of people dispossessed by the American government's failure to acknowledge its treaties of 1851–1852. I also do not know if there are people up there today from that group who might remember Minnie Bell's family or if that was just a name she got from a missionary. Around the Gold Rush country, white people called Indians whatever they pleased—as individuals and as groups. Just as these people were not "Bidwell's Indians," my great-grand-mother was probably not really "Minnie Bell." In fact, one of Pauline's aunts was named Minnie Belle Evans, and sometimes I wonder if someone tacked a name on her as if she were a blank slate without a name of her own. Pauline claimed that she did not know her mother's name and never spoke of her mother's side of the family. Pauline was able, as an old woman, to pass for white, but when she was younger, it was more difficult, judging from the pictures. My learning who her mother was—Minnie Bell—was literally from a deathbed "confession" Pauline made when I visited her in the hospital after the first of several strokes that would kill her within a day or two after my visit. It seemed important to her to tell me these things, and she also told her son, Dick Edwards. He was shocked and followed her example—he mentioned

what she said and never spoke of it again. A few years later, it was disclosed to me that there was a possibility that Dick Edwards, my mother's husband, might be my biological father. I remember the exact time I was told this—late December 1985 just before leaving for a conference in New York City. Someone who had obviously been making love to Coyote the night before chose to challenge me about who my father was. At the time, I was still reeling from the shock of not being sure anymore who was who in my family or who I was if I was not the person I had believed myself to be the day before I was told about Dick.

Men on horseback. If Dick Edwards was my father, the man on the left would be my great-grandfather, Frank Lee Evans, Pauline's father. He is on one of the horses he bred near the lava beds where Captain Jack, leader of a Modoc rebellion in northeastern California, and a few Modoc men held off the U.S. Army for a period of time after the U.S. government tried to force them to restrict their movements to reservation boundaries. My husband, Arthur, says that I am the family karma kickback. I guess it's true, because the deeper I delve into the various family histories, the more I find that the people from whom I come were the perpetrators of those very acts that ignited my rage (and my art). But then perhaps that is why such a family ends up with someone like me. I should emphasize the word "end"—neither my

brother nor I have had children. We represent the end of an entire branch of several families. Karma kickback—we ended it forever. This is one of those stories. It is likely that Frank or his father, Joseph Evans, supplied horses to the U.S. military to fight Kintpush (Captain Jack) because the U.S. Army was said to have been his best customer for horses. The family was still involved with breeding horses right down to my generation. My childhood was fairly evenly divided between going to school in the East Bay (Richmond and El Cerrito) near Berkeley and being on the ranch that my grandmother Pauline had with her husband then, Ivy Bell (no relation to her mother, Minnie Bell), outside of Chico. I was on a horse before I could walk. I know everybody says that, but it was really true. Somewhere I have a picture.

Mary Isabel Graham, my great-great-grand-
mother (if Dick Edwards was my father) with
an unidentified baby. Mary Isabel was the
mother of Frank Lee Evans and grandmother of
Pauline. She came west on a wagon train.
People who know me well know that I love
science fiction and fantasy literature and media.
They will appreciate the fun I had finding out
that Mary Isabel's family wagon train from
Missouri was led by one "Captain James Kirk."

Mary Isabel Graham and Joseph Evans, my great-great-grandparents, if Dick Edwards was my father. Joseph Evans was born in Kentucky in 1833, and Mary Isabel Graham was born in Missouri. They are Pauline Evans's grandparents. I am struck whenever I see these kinds of studio portraits of people from Ireland and Scotland. They seem to be unhappy and stern, so mean, so wounded. Sometimes people defend the subjects' apparent emotional state by talking about the physical discomfort they were feeling in sitting for a portrait in those days, but I see pictures from the same period of people from other nationalities who do not have such an austere, severe look. But perhaps it is that heritage of cold and wind against the standing stones. I have heard that if it were not for the Gulf Stream, the British Isles would have the climate of Alaska. I think "pioneer" pictures like this exemplify the "itch" that I recognize on the part of the immigrants. The other part of the "itch," of course, is on the part of the Natives and we who descend from the loving and unloving clashes between the two.

Me as a schoolgirl. In spite of the Pueblo Revolt of 1680, I was raised Catholic. Of course, I was not raised at Hopi but with my mother and Dick Edwards, who may or may not be my father, just as Charles Loloma may or may not be my father. These days when people ask what tribe I am, I still generally say that my father is Hopi because it's what I feel is correct and it's the only knowledge I had for a long time. I look like Charles Loloma, and he has spoken of me to some of his close friends; but it is also true that I did not live there and do not speak Hopi. I do not have a Hopi mother; therefore, even if Charles Loloma is my father, I am not Hopi. I do not have a clan because I do not have a Hopi mother. If Dick Edwards is my father, I know even less of who I am. Who were "Bidwell's Indians"? There was a Chico-Durham Rancheria— is that where they went when Chico State College took over the land where they had their homes? The little girl in the picture is about seven or eight years old—I can tell by the uniform because around the third grade, it was changed from dark brown to plaid. The nuns at school were all from Great Britain; one of them was a war hero who had saved the lives of many people during the London blitzes. They called me "featherhead" and thought I was stupid and slow. I was actually nearly blind, a fact no one caught until I was eight years old. But the reputation of being slow stuck all the way through the middle of the tenth grade (by then in public school); at that point I dropped out.

My mother, Betty Webb, as a very young woman. She was married in 1938, but I was not born until ten years later, three years after my brother. My mother was in her thirties when she had her children, unusual for her generation. When she was between eighteen and twenty, she did some local modeling for department stores; I have seen newspaper clippings of her. She was thin and would fit in with today's standards of beauty except that she was short. She was a little bit taller than I am; my height is 5 feet 3½ inches. My mother was a fine-boned, slender reed; I am (as one tourbook about Hopi country put it) "a little brown brick."

Dick Edwards, one of the two men who may or may not be my father, as a young man. He was a musician. He always loved classical music and opera, but became a professional trumpet and coronet player in the big bands. Several of my mother's friends who knew her then have told me that she met Charles Loloma when Dick Edwards was away for an extended period of time for a musical gig. This must have been in 1947. It is not clear to me who was where, because she traveled in the Southwest—especially around Utah—and Charles was on the West Coast at some point just after the war. Neither has volunteered the details. Dick Edwards was born in 1914 in Colusa, California, and died in 1996.

Arthur Murata and family—
Toshio Murata, his father, and
Fujiko Yamamoto, his strong-
willed, independent mother.
Arthur is my husband of twenty-
six years as of March 2002.
Arthur is Sansei, third generation
in America. Both of his parents
were born in the San Francisco
Bay area but were sent to Japan
for their education while young
and did not return until they
were grown. Technically, they
are Nisei, second-generation
Americans, but also "kibei"—
returnees to California from
Japan. When they returned it
was as if they were first-time
immigrants in terms of language
and culture. They spoke broken
English all their lives and always
found it easier to write in
Japanese than in English. Arthur
spoke only Japanese at home
until he was seven years old, but

after he began to attend school and learn English, the Japanese faded into the
background to the point where today he says he does not really speak or
understand Japanese. It is an object lesson to those of our Native people who
are fortunate enough to have been raised in a home where they have kept
their own language. Do not let your children lose it. Because even if they
speak nothing else as children, it is still possible for it to be "lost" when they
get older. When I met Arthur, he was a professional magician in San Francisco

and a judo instructor, currently holding a fifth-degree black belt. Today we have a store specializing in science fiction, fantasy, and Japanese anime collectibles in Fresno, California, called "Oh Grow Up," a name that Arthur thought up driving along a winding lakeside road near Coarsegold. Being unusual runs in the family: His mother juggled and his father ran the still at Topaz, Utah, where both of them were imprisoned during World War II.

Charles Loloma, the man who is most likely my father and whom I have always regarded as such, with a younger, thinner me in front of his home in Hotevilla, 1977. Charles Loloma was a well-known artist, although I didn't know that about him for a long time after I first began to visit Hopi to see him. I still have a silver bracelet, once set with four pieces of malachite, that he gave to my mother—one of his earliest pieces. He was Badger Clan from his mother, my grandmother, Rachel. His grandfather (my great-grandfather, Lololomai) was one of the main people involved in the famous split between the "friendly" and the "hostile" factions in Oraibi. The split led to the founding of Hotevilla, where Charles lived until his death in 1991. When I would visit, I always cried when I left. It felt like my arms were being torn from their sockets or my heart from inside my body to leave. And yet I never spent one night in his home. It was he who told me that there was really no place for me at Hopi since my mother was not a Hopi. Until recently, I did not name him when people asked who my father was, even though he freely told a number of people about me. When I would visit, various relatives would introduce me to their children as "Auntie" and talk about how much I looked like Charles, but the fact remained that daughters and fathers at Hopi do not have the kind of relationship that exists among Anglos in America.

Without a Hopi mother, there was no maternal uncle to fill that spot, just as Charles was such a person for his nieces and nephews. Today I feel I was wrong in not being more open about him from the beginning. I think I left the impression with some people that I was just a "wannabe" when I did not name my father. When I learned how famous he was, I was afraid that if I named him, people would think I just wanted his money (and he had quite a lot) or to associate myself with his fame. It really was not until I learned that there was a possibility that he was not my father that I decided to "come out" and just state the facts as I knew them.

About the Author

Wendy Rose was born in 1948 in Oakland, California, and grew up in the Bay Area. She has participated in First Nations issues and events since 1958 and teaches American Indian Studies at Fresno City College. She lives in Coarsegold, California (halfway between Fresno and Yosemite), in the foothills of the Sierra Nevada with her husband, Arthur Murata, and an ever-changing assortment of creatures who permit her to live on their land. Her house is about thirty miles from the place where her European and Miwok ancestors lived, the Europeans having been forty-niners in the Gold Rush. Wendy and Arthur also operate a small store in Fresno called Oh Grow Up that specializes in science fiction, fantasy, and Japanese merchandise.